W0114035

THE NAMING

African
POETRY
BOOK SERIES

Series editor: Kwame Dawes

EDITORIAL BOARD

Chris Abani, Northwestern University

Gabeba Baderoon, Pennsylvania
State University

Kwame Dawes, University of
Nebraska–Lincoln

Phillippa Yaa de Villiers, University
of the Witwatersrand

Bernardine Evaristo, Brunel
University London

Aracelis Girmay

John Keene, Rutgers University

Matthew Shenoda, Brown University

ADVISORY BOARD

Laura Sillerman

Glenna Luschei

Sulaiman Adebowale

Elizabeth Alexander

THE NAMING

Chinụa Ezenwa-Ọhaeto

University of Nebraska Press | Lincoln

© 2025 by the Board of Regents of
the University of Nebraska

Acknowledgments for the use of copyrighted material appear on
pages xi–xiii, which constitute an extension of the copyright page.

The African Poetry Book Series is operated by the African
Poetry Book Fund. The APBF was established in 2012 with
initial support from philanthropists Laura and Robert
F. X. Sillerman. The founding director of the African
Poetry Book Fund is Kwame Dawes, Holmes University
Professor and Glenna Luschei Editor of *Prairie Schooner*.

All rights reserved

The University of Nebraska Press is part of a land-grant
institution with campuses and programs on the past, present, and
future homelands of the Pawnee, Ponca, Otoe-Missouria, Omaha,
Dakota, Lakota, Kaw, Cheyenne, and Arapaho Peoples, as well as
those of the relocated Ho-Chunk, Sac and Fox, and Iowa Peoples.

For customers in the EU with safety/GPSR concerns, contact:
gpsr@mare-nostrum.co.uk
Mare Nostrum Group BV
Mauritskade 21D
1091 GC Amsterdam
The Netherlands

Library of Congress Cataloging-in-Publication Data
Names: Ezenwa-Ọhaeto, Chinụa author
Title: The naming / Chinụa Ezenwa-Ọhaeto.
Other titles: Naming (Compilation)
Description: Lincoln: University of Nebraska Press,
2025. | Series: African poetry book series
Identifiers: LCCN 2025008554
ISBN 9781496244703 paperback
ISBN 9781496245465 epub
ISBN 9781496245472 pdf
Subjects: BISAC: POETRY / African | LCGFT: Poetry
Classification: LCC PR9387.9.E94476 N36 2025
LC record available at https://lccn.loc.gov/2025008554

Set in Garamond Premier Pro by L. Welch.
Designed by N. Putens.

For

Dad, the Man we called Ezenwa-Ọhaeto

For

Mum, the Woman we call Ngozi Ezenwa-Ọhaeto

And for

Fellow champion, the Siblings we call

Nnedimma, Onyedikachukwu, and Uchechukwu

So much there is we must atone
—KOFI AWOONOR

I stand at the threshold
. . . undoing the knots of silence
—'GBENGA ADEOBA

CONTENTS

ACKNOWLEDGMENTS

I am grateful to my ancestors, especially Ọbashị and his offspring, without whom none of this would have been possible. Our fathers' fathers, the homestead is well and in safekeeping with us, your descendants. To my mother, stupendous love. Huge, huge love to my wife, Mmesoma, whose belief, trust, and encouragement are a halo over my head. A heartfelt gratitude to Kwame Dawes for his guidance, for the right path of this work, and for reminding me what it means to remember.

Boundless thanks to my Kindred, for always showing me kindness: De Akunnia Chijioke Tassie, Da Eunice Edo, De Ejike Ọhaeto, De Ugochukwu Ọhaeto, De Amarachi Ndubuisi, De Obi Ọhaeto, Da Ngozi Ọhaeto, De Sam Chukwunyere, De Anozie Chukwunyere, De Dwayne Nmezi, De Onyedikachi Nmezi, De Tony Ebosie, De Muna Tassie, Uncle Obinna Ezedinobi Ngejeme, Grandma Née Mary-Magdalene Ngejeme, Aunty Chinelo Adilih, Aunty Uche and Amarachi Tim-Agu, Aunty Chinelo Onwuka, Uncle Onyedika and Aunty Lilian Mgbeokwere.

Also, thank you to my professors and friends, Rev. Fr. Obi Josephat Oguejiofor, Remi Raji, Lydia Kim, Franca Nwogu, Ifeyinwa Ogbazi, Olisa Eloka, Kathryn Kysar, Kelechi Chibuikem, Uche Peter Umezurike, Tolulokpe Oke, Sueddie Agema, Unoma Azuah, Samuel Ugbechie, Rasaq M. Gbolahan, Amu Nnadi, Elizabeth Tussey, Segun and Ibk Oladipo, Bestman Michael, Elliot

Uguru, Abuchi Modilim, Darlington Chibueze Anuonye, Molara Wood, Delight C. Ejiaka, Lyette Erin, Zainab A. Omaki, Ngozi M. Emmanuel, and Joshua Effiong for the solid support.

A special thank you to Matthew Shenoda and Chigozie Obioma for always giving me a listening ear. And to Chike Okoye, Chika Unigwe, Patrice Nganang, Onyebuchi Ile, and Akua Agyeiwaa Manieson for those insightful and energetic words. And to Ikhide Ikheloa, Emmanuel Audu and Daniel Egbebunmi for their support. Nneka Osakwe, thank you.

My deep gratitude to Chimezie Chika for the discussions and seeing the early drafts of this work. Thanks to Eduardo C. Corral, Timothy Schaffert and Ng'ang'a Wahu-Muchiri for all the assistance. Thanks to Ber Anena, the awesome friend, for the kind words. Thanks to my cousins: Chibuzo and Chinonso Aniebonam for giving me everything I needed when I arrived at Lincoln. Bibi Ukonu, thank you. I am grateful.

And thanks to the editors of the following publications, in which some poems, under different titles and versions, originally appeared:

20.35 Africa
Dgeku Magazine
Efiko
Frontier Poetry
LitMag
Lolwe
Malahat Review
Massachusetts Review
Notre Dame Review
Oxford Poetry
Palette Poetry
Poetry Ireland Review
Unbound: An Unthology of New Nigerian Poets Under 40
Up the Staircase Quarterly

A thank you to the entire editorial board of African Poetry Book Series, for their support. I am also grateful to the English Department of the University of Nebraska–Lincoln for the space that enabled me to understand my work better.

This is for you dear reader, thanks for understanding and recognizing this work's beauty.

Dàálú!

THE NAMING

OUR FATHERS'
FATHERS

A hoodie hangs
on the outside of
a shop down the street
and I wonder about the face(s)
it will conceal.

A Call at Dawn

Dear kinsman, Nwanne m,
bear with me for calling you up at this hour.

I must tell that there is a monkey's
hand asking for our hands and heads.

This monkey's hand is monkeying us badly.
As you can see, I do not possess the full skills to handle it alone.
It would be great if we put our hands and heads together against the
monkey's hand monkeying us badly, and unclench its
fingers one after the other which are fisting us in many ways.

Dear kinsman, I am here by way of dialogue and imploration.
To un-monkey the monkey's hand, let's show our itches and the wounds on our flag;
let's un-tiger and rabbit and lever everything clawing at our progress and history.

I used to hide thinking I was doing me well.
It took me very long to understand what made
the prodigal son return to his father was maturity.

I do not want the things that happened to the prodigal
son to also happen to us before we realize ourselves.

Look at me, Nwanne m, I have carried enough gashes and darkness;
the *ékwè* slit drum from the square back home and our flag is sounding for our action,
let's question the ridges stationed on our bills, lands, memories, and past and present
and future by going to the homestead and asking our fathers' fathers for assistance.

II

Dear kinsman, remember our fathers often say
when a secret lingers for long, even the deaf hear it.
Let's ask our fathers' fathers the things it takes to unravel the things we can't resolve.
Let's ask our fathers' fathers for guidance, for what they know.

III

Dear kinsman, Nwanne m, we must call on our fathers' fathers.
To begin, here are the things required:
Kòlà. Ńzụ̀. Palm wine. And Alligator pepper.
Items for each market day mooning our lineage and history.
Items for libations, offerings and incantations to show our respect.

Dear kinsman, we must call our fathers' fathers
because they are part of the hands and heads we need
to handle the monkey's hand monkeying us badly.

Let's call on them to know why we are turning into dry bones in our bowl,
why our robins crack in their chirps, why our roads eat us,
why we carry too many memories that are heavier than our backs,
why our anthem teeth us down, why our home is turning into a distant light,
why the institutions are shoveled in the neck, why the leaders
are flooding the states, mangling our faces, and shitting on us.

My hands are steady, full of ablutions.
My eyes are steady too, well with supplications.

Dear kinsman, Nwanne m, we must wade firmly to bring us off the sea storm.
Now, we call on our fathers' fathers . . .

O please, kinsman, please, put your ringing phone on silent.

IV

Nwanne m, now we are here,
let's bow our heads as we begin:

Our fathers' fathers, we have come.
Like good children, we have come.

As we kneel, our hands are full of gifts and respect, please accept them.
We have come as always, carrying with us questions.

It's the Òrìè market day, today, and the sky smiles well upon us.
You told us the fly that eats with care follows the meat to its origin.

And here we are, our fathers' fathers, treading with care and reverence.
We have not been conscious enough of our doings, please redirect and direct us.

We carry in our hands a plate of eagerness, we want our hurtings disarmed.
We want to understand the things we don't fully understand.

When a thing deems itself difficult, the child looks for the father. That's why we are here.
You see far, near, beyond, and beneath, our fathers' fathers, things our eyes
and mortal bodies can't reach. That's why we are here.

There is a monkey's hand in our midst, our fathers' fathers.
The monkey's hand is monkeying us badly.

We beseech you, our fathers' fathers,
give us the needed to un-monkey the monkey's hand monkeying
us badly, and even the monkey's hand yet to monkey us:
the knowledge, functions, discourse, and thoughts
as we, full of our differentness and itches, unfurl our memories,
past, present, future, worries and questions before you.

Our fathers' fathers,
do hear us.

                              Dear kinsman, Nwanne m,
                              I will go first.

Appraisal

Our fathers' fathers, I am thankful,
for all you fought for, the blessings we now enjoy.
We adore and adorn you with the appellation
of the leopard killers. It is well deserved and much more.
It is said that when one who does a wonderful
thing is appreciated, he feels the eagerness to do another.
We are grateful for everything, our fathers' fathers.
And may I not grow boils in the mouth when words are needed from me.
We, your great-great-great-great-grandchildren, remain grateful.

Our fathers' fathers, this is me once more saying that an invitation
is nothing like the prophetic ululation an ukulele could never produce.
And I have understood since Eri, the founder of the Igbo
people, that what is agreed upon and not done is dust.
Our fathers' fathers, for long the alert drum has been
sounding from the square and our flag, and with each
passing day, the sounding gets louder, calling on our attention.

The monkey's hand is monkeying us badly.
The monkey's hand is an enemy.

Our fathers' fathers, you have never allowed an enemy to laugh at us.
But the enemy is saying many bad things about us now.

They say we do not know what we are doing,
but in the sun I am making a shirt out of its rays.

They say we do not know what we are doing,
but when people put up land for sale, we buy them.

They say we do not know what we are doing,
but our Afrobeats and Nollywood are becoming great industries.

They say we do not know what we are doing,
but we go into spaces and places with our writings and Ìzàgà.

They say we do not know what we are doing,
but our kindred's children are doing marvelously in the universities.

They say we do not know what we are doing,
but you taught us how to be in two places at the same time.

They say we do not know what we are doing,
but we are in innovations and donate the most in gatherings.

They say we do not know what we are doing,
but in every Ìkèjì festival, we untie the ram.

They say we do not know what we are doing,
but no masquerade is as big and highly decorated as our Ìjelè.

They say we do not know what we are doing,
but ụmụ Obashi are trading and doing great things in many places.

They say we do not know what we are doing,
but we never put God or any God in a difficult position.

Our fathers' fathers, it is known that the strength
of a people is resident in their number;
our enemy, the monkey's hand, is growing in number.

Do not let the enemy laugh at us,
do not let the monkey's hand do to us bad-bad things.

Unfurling

I greet you, Chukwu Ọ̀kị̀ké, God of all existence, here is kòlà
to thank you for life, good health, and opportunities.

To you my Chi, I give this kòlà, asking you
to present my requests anywhere they matter.

I greet you, our fathers' fathers—
Ikaigbo, Ishigbo, Owèrrè, Ishiowèrrè, Idụma,
Ọbashị, Ibegwa, Ọhaeto, Ogbonna, Ezenwa—
you never leave our side. I give you kòlà.

I greet our dear land, the stronghold of everything below the sun, here is kòlà.
I greet those who live above, those who live in the middle, and those who
    live below. Kòlà.
I greet this country and hope that someday it will know better. Kòlà.
I greet our enemies, for it is good never to leave anyone behind. Kòlà.

Dear kinsman, Nwanne m, here is kòlà.

Our fathers' fathers,
masters of astral travel, bilocation, and shapeshifting,
see me. I am here and have been walking with my darkness.
I have been in the corner with rotten pears in my mouth.
I have spoken so much about the heavy memories in my bones.
I have spoken so much about my disturbances that I wonder if anyone listens.
Here is to the future that translates my failures.
The hurt in my chest holding my nameable scars yearns for a garden of flowers.
Our fathers' fathers, it's such a long time since I called myself in our language.

I have been asking around to know our people well, to find our right hand.
My emptying pockets reveal my struggles before I can speak of them.
I am young, so young, and do not want the monkey's hand monkeying me to death.
I want to be together with my rabbits.
I want to be together with my shards.
I was born in Àfò day, and the earth is my element.
There is hunger in my wants. There is hunger in my mouth.
There are monsters in this country, they are teething me everywhere.
And some dreams keep swimming away from me, swimming away from my grasp.
Our fathers' fathers, I know sometimes my face gnaws at the light;
do listen as I keep naming the monkey's hand monkeying me badly.

Naming

I leave my bed every day to search
for the steadiness in my memories and history's anachronisms.
I gather the borders of my body
so as not to miss the July rain dropping on dusty roofs.
I have been thinking so much about the
monkey's hand and how it digs into me.
I have been thinking so much about how we are a sad generation
with happy photographs on social media.
I want to understand what I cannot hear.
I want to hear what I cannot understand.
And for some time now, I have noticed that people's eyes,
heated with the flame of their passion, glow
differently when they talk about their dreams.

I have known many longings, and the openings on my
skin keep letting out my prayers.
I grow flowers and ask them to name me
as we named them—this is shared power.
I have said many things about people I love
so that I can be found easily whenever I get lost.

Dear country, my place of birth,
I am staring at your chest.
I will name the ugly things in there together
with your tiger claws clawing me badly: the kidnappings, the lootings,
the unreviewed bills, the subjugating laws, the hike in prices, the lawlessness . . .

I kiss our surname to track my first name back in history.
I look into history to point out the places where it leaks.
My father taught me to always recognize the enigma in ablutions,
and since then, I have been locking my body with precedents,
un-flaunting my lips at time. I want to learn
how to think less of the things I cannot own. I want to learn
enough patience so I can count the hairs
gathering on my testicles. I want to learn
the secrets children keep with their parents. Even when there are none.

Our people often say that a corpse appears like a log of wood
to someone who is not related to the deceased. Therefore, I do
not take everything about life for granted, not even death.

My sister gives me feathers in the mornings:
she wants me to see what our worrying doesn't look like.

Marley's Lyrics in Two Parts or Where Does It Hurt the Most?

—after the Igbo Landing, 1803

PART ONE

I

At Dunbar Creek on St. Simons Island, Georgia,
your voices our fathers' fathers still sing,
Home. Home is where we belong;
Water Spirits will take us home.
Sometimes history is cruel, and in this
moment, I imagine that when you were moored in the
Schooner York heading to Dunbar by the sea, the fishes
that heard your wailings shocked at their fins and pectorals;
above the sea, the seagulls that flew past took to the sea waves
the horrible things they saw happening to you.
Even the wind itself bore witness. And Roswell King,
with his own eyes during the landing,
saw 75 bodies in the openings of history.

II

You were great elephants of our lands, our fathers' fathers,
and refused to be wrongly named, wrongly placed;
refused to be the property of Couper and Spalding.
You understood the weight of knowledge and courage
and chose not to be transactions—priced at $100 each for forced labor.
Our fathers' fathers, you chose not to be taken less, not to be forgotten.

III

If I could, I would accost the deck of the *Schooner York* that
held you, our fathers' fathers, to hear how it succumbed to
your bravery, to the kindred spirit that stirred
your bones, the unyielding chants that rose from your throats.
I want to know everything about you because knowing
arms me well enough to not forget where the tiger rain
started beating history and where it stopped.

PART TWO

IV

Òfò, my uncle, one evening told me how
his great-great-great-uncle left one day and never returned.
And word had it he was captured, chained, iron-marked on the chest
and turned into the property of one Mr. Winterbottom or Mr. John Hawkins.
History is a privilege and volumes and volumes of poetry.
I can only imagine the immense burden it placed upon
my uncle's great-great-great-uncle's father on
receiving words about his son: the heaviness. The bitterness. The agony.
For days, he lingered by the door, waiting for his son's return.

V

In my mother's place of birth, a story goes that one Ada Ezeigwe lost
her arm at Badagry port, tearing it free from the shackles that bound her.
She refused to be owned, to be a thing at a master's command.
The story has it she died from blood loss while running for safety.
I imagine her blood, its trails up to the point where she collapsed, screaming,
I refuse to be chained. I refuse to be taken.

VI

I go to the shores of our village river,
searching for the memories it holds.
I go to the shores of our village river
and pointing at history—
I want to know where it hurts the most.

What I Said to God, Chukwu Ọ̀kịké

God touched me.
And I said: *I want to know*
where it hurts the most
so I can take care of it;
it's been a while now
something good happened to me.
I tried to pray, to read my lobes of kòlà, to
show how my body could stretch again.
Sometimes, one has to lose
to understand oneself, you know?
Nobody wants an amateur.
Not even God. Not even you, Nwanne m.
I seek the underside of progress
for the many months my bed couldn't piece
me together like a jigsaw puzzle.
I was not born for this gloominess I carry.
I hold the day because it saw the night.
Then, I touched God's nose, and there
was laughter nestling on my palms.
Then I said: *I did not come to you by chance,*
let this strangeness not stamp me out of your eyes.

The Story of Chinụalụmọgụ Not Looking for Anything with His Lazy Eyes

I cherish the moment I awaken each morning
to find myself beside my wife, as if for the first time.

I live in a period when people no longer understand patience.
But I know what it means, for it is said that
a man with patience is favored and a fortunate one—
and understands there is nothing beautiful in a history's blackout.

The yams and cassava in our farm planted by my hands begs the soil
for the meaning in the gaps of movement and living,
begs for the meaning of my handling and think I do not know, but I know.

My sister has been a handle to my growth.
When we were children, she taught me how to play cook with
tins found in trash cans and how to tend to babies made of discarded cloth.
Without my sister, I wouldn't have known what it means to sibling,
to childhood and brim with stars; I wouldn't have known
what it means to stretch out a hand in the dark and find.

Everything changes—this I know. But what exactly
changes everything? The story of me not looking
for anything with my lazy eyes goes that I actually do not have
lazy eyes but possess a particular way of not risking the things I see.

Everything and everyone and every day keep combing my body
so that it knows well enough and long enough, both fullness and loss.

Memorabilia

One night after I turned 19 years old, I dreamt.
I was sitting in a bar with my father.
We rattled about the reeds at home and the things he had missed.
When I looked him in the eyes, I found the shrinking thing.

The first time I saw the shrinking thing was when he
had been down with cancer and looked eaten from the inside.
He started growing distant. Each day, my father was gradually
pulled away from me, from us. Then he traveled.
Toward health. Toward work. Toward Cambridge.
He was a father and had to do fatherly things.
And that was the last time he sent me to buy some newspapers,
sent me to wash his car, sent me to clean his boots.

At 30, I saw my father again in my dream;
I told him that people, on hearing what I do, often say,
In this country, you mean you are a poet?
My father smiled at me after listening and said,
Flowers never grow knives; the world can only adjust for you.

Today, I am in my father's jacket. Putting it on feels like I
am having a conversation with him, like we are in a field, holding hands
and watching butterflies bounce in the air and land on Calla Lilies.

What Chinụalụmọgụ Made with Clouds

When I was 8 and ostentatious,
I used to sit outside the house
and watch the clouds, and then make what I deemed fit
with a battalion of them floating across the sky.
Once, it was a man smiling that I made and his smile was clean as spring.
I wanted to be the man just to be him.
Another time, it was half-jawed monsters I made with the clouds:
I watched them move slowly from one side
in the sky to another till they disappeared.
That day, the monsters gave me a hot chase in my dream.
In the morning, my sister told me I talked in my sleep.
And on walking away, she said,
there must be something about talking and sleeping.
What I got from her words was that we can't always
control the things we carry inside of us.
Another day, my friends popped out on the clouds,
and we talked about our class teacher and school, hide-and-seek and girls.
We talked about how we pressed neighbors' doorbells and took off;
how we trapped lizards in tins and caught grasshoppers
with our palms; how we played Yokozuna, Goldberg,
Bam Bam Bigelow and the Undertaker; how we played under the rain
and caked thereafter with mud under our feet.
We talked about everything and almost nothing
till I couldn't see them anymore.
When I started seeing two persons locking lips in the clouds,
I knew my neighbor's daughter who lived
down the street was doing something to me.
It was obvious because for long I had been looking

through the windows to see her walk past.
One day, I stood upon my shyness, walked
to my neighbor's daughter and said, *hi*.
She didn't look to see what I looked like,
didn't halt, and didn't turn around.
It seemed there were eyes following her, shielding
her from speaking to people on the street.
The next time I saw people locking lips in the clouds, I aimed a big
stone, the size of an adult rabbit, at it.
I threw the stone from the chaos sitting in my heart.
At 13, I survived a loss that saw me to the dark,
cancer had its way to my father's colon. It has been
many years now since the loss, and today looking up at the sky,
I saw my father in the clouds. He smiled at me.
His teeth were sharp and his smile wide and clear like an ocean full of seagulls.
At that moment, I discovered my tenderness and resolve.

Once Upon a Time the Teeth

The story about my milk teeth
that controlled my innocence goes that
at 5, during a play with my friends, a thrown
punch got two milk teeth off my mouth.
I watched them sail through the air and land on the ground.
I gathered them up and threw them onto the house zinc—
a thing children do in this place where we are from.
I begged lizards, the tooth fairies of our people, to go for them
because they would give me better teeth.
Perhaps, the ones I could use to trounce bones and decimate stones.
Many weeks came and passed, and the better teeth emerged,
and I learned many different things to do with them.
I learned how to fake toothaches so I could gain more care
from my parents than I normally received.
I learned how to drill at night perfect tiny holes
in packets of juice and milk stored in the fridge, and got
packaging companies blamed when questioned beyond my lies and tears.
I discovered I could win fights by leaving
behind teeth marks, as gifts and emblems, on skin.
My teeth did much and even contemplated arrogance.
Now, my teeth have become a portrait of margins calling
out the werewolves gnawing at my existence's moon.

The Navel

One evening, when I was 9 years old,
I walked into the kitchen and said to my mother,
Mum, why is my navel this big?
My playmates laugh at me, calling it weird.
On the streets, they stare and stare, mum,
like I am carrying something that shouldn't be with me.
My mother looked at me, smiled, bent, and said,
Son, you're not different; you remind everyone that someone
took care of them before they could do so for themselves.
You remind everyone how cups always hold teas whether cold or hot.
My mother patted me on the back, then handed me a pack of chocolate
and walked me into the living room where I sat and played *Ncho* and then
Devil May Cry on my PlayStation 2. Looking at my navel now
and revisiting the words my mother said to me,
I have no choice but to recall the theories and galleries of distort I heard
over the years from meeting people who carry a navel the size of mine.
One, I remember, told me, *I feel like I carry a small moon.*
Another said, *in every room I enter, it owls out, stumbles, and shies away.*
Another said, *my navel details fire on faces before pocketing it.*
I must confess, our fathers' fathers, that these are navels in the glories.
Navels of the holies. Navels with the stories.
There's no better period to be born than the period I was born;
no better way to be born than this way.
My navel is yes yes yes to the family that made me from love;
is yes yes to the goodbyes in cupcakes and masks;
and is yes to the bad words terrified of my kindness and elegance.

Here

Phase 1
Our fathers' fathers.
Here, my triumph is to understand my hunger.
This hunger has been about the dusky sky, the past, and this lilting world,
about myself, the present, and the things I am yet to become.
I set my hunger down on an operation table and direct the light
into its oubliette. If not for anything else, I want to satisfy my questions.
Questions are crossroads where something is taken and something is left behind.

Phase 2
Here, my silence is a church where I am not a worshipper.
My silence once said to me, what you can't touch doesn't belong to you.
My silence once said to me, what you can't see isn't what you want.
I want to kiss the rippling life inside and outside of my expectations.
But then, look at how the terror we create pokes everything beautiful.

Phase 3
Here, I am not sure about the length of my dreams
and how much longer I am to hold on to them.
In my forgetfulness, I still build a pyre for my wounds.
I have a pen. I have a piece of paper and also a small mirror,
I write to myself because it's a way
I can tell what my name means—a garden of empathic mirth.

The Actual Story About the Keloid
on Chinụalụmọgụ's Left Arm

I told my mother one of the stories
because I wanted her to believe I got it
from falling off a fence and tearing my skin.
My mother told this story to her friends who
asked about the keloid at different times they set
their feet on the roads leading to our house.
I also told my friends another story about the
keloid which they told their friends who had asked
me about it and I refused to open my mouth to them.
The actual story about the keloid on my left arm
goes that I was bitten by a dog from the next compound
on the evening I jumped over the fence to pick some leaves
for mock soup play. I was 6. No, 7. I think I was either 9 or 8.
The keloid has become the stories it once wasn't
and the many other stories that followed.
I look at the keloid now and I am reminded of the color black.
I am about three decades old and I now see
black not as a color, but as an absence.
An absence of every other color.
Our fathers' fathers, looking at the keloid,
I also see the absence of childhood,
the absence of open wound, the absence of deductions, and,
somehow, the absence of tears the dog bite brought to my
eyes, excepting the pain it caused.
The keloid on my arm has become a map of memory,
a small hill and a shiny dome of exigency: and has
toned deeper my skin color where it sits.

Running my fingers across the keloid, I realize it is not
a shame (or blame) and something that
does not give an outline for what isn't living in it.
Running my fingers across the keloid,
I see a history that gives an outline so as not to be forgotten.

Colors

Our fathers' fathers,
I have a story about colors:

In this story, I am 29 and watching my nephew fill
his picture book with crayons. It's like witnessing allomorphs
doing their things with morphemes. He breaks a crayon, then picks another.
He reminds me of when I was his age—it was late evening and
my picture book was filled with dinosaurs: the kinds I saw in the movies
and would never see in real life. I held a yellow crayon and
used it all over an outlined Styracosaurus. I was crayoning carefully
so I wouldn't miss a spot. I wanted the filling spaces sunny and bright like a desert.
Yellow reminds me of this village: its golden afternoons merge
people with their shadows and dents,
and the corrugated rooftops bellow their half-dreams.

Green crayon. I wrapped my fingers around a green
crayon into position and ran it over an outlined Allosaurus.
Green reminds me of my family's farm which is no more.
My family's farm got eaten by spillages—
the carelessness of people with big torchlights.
My family's farm: hectares of plants and vegetables and trees; hectares of greens.
My family's farm had cassava ridges, cocoyam ridges,
and mounds with sprouting corns. It also had an Obeche tree—
the lady of circumference, space, and shade—amongst other trees,
which I was fond of because my aunt told me the tree was planted by
my great-great-grandfather, Ibegwa, whom everyone believed I don't look like.

When done with the green crayon, I picked a red one. And ran
it over the body of an outlined Velociraptor. Though I did not
like the red crayon or the red color, it brightened the picture book.
Red reminds me of blood, like the one I saw on the television
during a news hour. A terrible sight it was: a group of masked
individuals videoed themselves unhooking a head from its
body, then blood pumped into the air. Pumping and pumping, just like that.
For a week, this scene filled me with nausea. Gave me a heavy head.
Red reminds me of my wounds like the one, now
keloids and a mark of presence and absence, I sustained
on falling off a mango tree and fences. Red reminds me of things:
anger, dying, crashes, openings, theorem of deduction . . .
But today, I try to think red as flowers,
as mornings full of yawns, scents, and calm.

Black. I picked a black crayon. Held it into position and ran it
over an outlined Ankylosaurus. It was almost night and crickets
were beckoning home parents, traders, drunkards, gossipers, travelers . . .
Black is night to me; black is when I close my eyes to sleep, black reminds
me of the day I witnessed my sister's eyes fill with shock on connecting
her forehead with a wall during a play. Black is also like death to me,
because it reminds me of graves, graveyards, and emptiness.
I first experienced death when my grandmother died.
Then my grandfather. Then my father. Black reminds me of death:
black years, black memories. Black. Black crayon.
With black color, I have realized that to remain close to our dead,
we cherish images of them in our heads, pictures and videos.
Death makes us protest the fact of death.
Is there any logic to death, to grief, to after death?

I set down the black crayon when done. And looked at what
I did with the color. And the other colors.
The marvel I evoked with them evoked me.

The Gift

My Grandma before she died, before her bed
swallowed what was left behind on her skin,
gifted me a jar—blue and lined with white.
She said I would find life's disturbances inside it.
And that I should look inside and speak with it as often as I could
because it would enable me to gain the eyes to see whatever
is coming behind me. My grandma died many years ago.
Since then, I have experienced a lot of things which
I never saw coming: like a neighbor's dog that I took on a walk, it
broke off its leash and dashed for the grove; like the day I
woke up and heard my brother was hit by a motorbike;
like the day I studied for hours and failed an exam in one hour;
like last month when my inaccuracy caused my soccer team to a defeat;
like two weeks ago, my oversight at my job's inflow had me fired,
like yesterday while climbing down the stairs, I stumbled down
and broke my arm. So many things I didn't see coming.
I am holding the jar my grandma gifted me and trying
to figure out the ways I haven't found any life's disturbance
inside it; the ways I haven't spoken to it well enough to
understand why it has not yet enabled me to gain the eyes to see the
things that are coming behind me which have now done me a few damages.

Teaching My Nephew

My sister and her baby once homed
with me when I was a bachelor.
It was late evening, and it dawned on
us that we needed to placate our stomachs.
My sister handed me her baby
and went into the kitchen to make some food.
I had my sister's baby in my arms. And close to my chest.
My heartbeats beat him out of sleep.
I cuddled him so my sister would not think a pinch happened.
My sister worried a lot then. Maybe it was a thing that
came with having a baby for the first time.
My heart was always heavy; heavy with
the things I carried in this small life.
I wanted to teach her baby a thing or two
about the heavy things I carried.
Perhaps, teach him about gardens rounding a bush.
Or teach him that every one of my heartbeats is not a wince or a wound.
Or teach him how things are never straight; how things
could be flower one night and something else another night.
Or teach him that there are things that come with growing up;
but I knew he would not understand. and I could not speak *tah-tah-goo-goo-ga-ga*.
So I planted my thick lips on his cheek
and hoped it would teach him a thing or two instead.

There Is a New Philosophy Now
Called *Kwechiri, to Persevere*

Tomorrow is an unknown and circling like desert vultures.
Trying too hard to figure it out has been an albatross of my doing.
I know I am young, but I do not want the coming days appearing in shifts.

Kwechiri nwanne.

Every morning, I open my eyes hoping to be familiar
with what I have made of myself; hoping the black goat
which survived the night can recognize the kindness of the moon.

Kwechiri.

Look well, Nwanne m, at this country and hear its caring anthem.
I first looked at this country's flag the day I noticed my sister
checking at every moment if her sleeping baby still breathes.
No gree for anybody, sister. But, remember also that Keke driver
wey face trailer for road no dey shout "no gree for anybody."
Na die be that!

Kwechiri.

And because the chameleon is never afraid, and because when
the forest is accosted by heavy rain it never runs away, may I have its elegance
to chest the things life and its absurdities are throwing at me.
It took me long to find out that my vulnerability
is a voice wading through a storm.

Kwechiri.

There's so much to learn and no idea of what should not to be learned,
but it has never stopped me from jumping onto buses to
visit the towns where dogs bark throughout the night.
Tomorrow is an unknown and circling like desert vultures.

Our fathers' fathers, m kwechirisie ike.

The Measure of Lost Things

I am overwhelmed by the vibrant
and tangy taste of tangerines.
But in that taste, something is lost.
I have been searching for the lost
thing in places where ghosts live.

I ask horses about the leaves lost in the wind
and the footsteps lost on every arrival to know if
I have been looking for the lost thing in the wrong place.

Ever since I began searching for the lost thing,
I have never for once been completely satisfied;
yet, my garden is full of cocoyam and pumpkins.

Although I am still searching for the lost thing
in the taste of tangerines, I think what doesn't enter
through our wounds finds a way through our mouths.

Itches

I
As a little boy, I was taught that heroes are only
those who killed their enemies. I was taught many things
that now make it hard to sometimes know right from wrong.

II
One time, I came upon Ọhia river in this village,
and its shimmering face defied the illusions of erudition and hunger.
I was told rivers were places where people said goodbye to their families.
Rivers saw the whips and manacles that forced people into ships.
I have read and heard things about the memories a river can hold.
Standing by this river in our village, I wondered about the itches it
caused the families whose members were never seen again,
the number of people who were taken across it; the innocent people
who drowned in it—a thousand, or three thousand, or more.

III
In the handful of years I have spent on this earth, I know
that what people often overlook is the arrogance of itch,
especially when it strikes one squarely on the arse in the confines of
a moving bus packed with passengers. Every itch that itches is a kin that itches.
I want my courage to confront the itch that is itching me.

IV

Forgive my thoughts. Forgive them. But,
see how we sometimes invalidate everything that suffers;
see how we use tribalism to stuff stones into hungry mouths;
see how we live and think that nothing matters; that everything is *cruise*:
say Sars killings and kidnappings, say Asaba Massacre,
say Public Funds Lootings blamed on rodents;
say the media outside the continent only publish poverty stories about us.
I confess that this is a terrible time to be alive.

V

This is a terrible time to be alive.
The monkey's hand is doing us bad-bad things.
Our fathers' fathers, see the heaviness of our uncertainties.

The Robin in My Heart

a man who calls himself a god too soon often gets blinded by the moon
—OUR FATHERS' FATHERS

I sometimes wonder what my fingers mean.
I tame some of my ghosts to calm the storms in my life.
I get scared when I don't see my father in my dreams.
This is me affirming I will not be cut off young.

I listen to Burna Boy's *Common Person* because it allows
me the charm of knowing that every face deserves laughter,
that I should pet the robin that sings in my heart.

In my dear heart, I hold this country close.
But it breaks its people and keeps silence at
the dead bodies growing in the streets.

This country mangles and breaks its people,
and keeps unbuckling pitchforks on its citizens' bodies.

WORRIES

Our fathers' fathers, anytime I remember
Gracious David-West,

I cry. I cry for the bad-bad things he did:
the women he suffocated and killed.

And the hotels where he did the killings,
the beds, walls, floors.

I imagine the horrors of the dying,
the pleas from the women

before they were unlived.
I remember and become a torn paper.

Once Upon a Girl, a Place of History

—for Ishiowerre where my fathers' fathers lived and tendered

Girl is a place,
a place of history.

            Girl half-windows into her dreams:
            some nights unfold damp woods
            and clash into her sleep.

She is calm.
like a pond. Like an overfed child.
Like the desert wind swirling in a glass of wine.

            Girl knows the theory of hope handled wrongly.
            She is not an empty shell;
            nor an untimed call by the muezzin.

Girl is a home.
A home disturbed and undisturbed by passersby.
She is a home with ruffled hair;
with debris and rubble sitting and un-sitting in her marrow.

            Girl is a collage of faces and
            technologies. Also a garden with lamplights.

Girl takes out a cigarette and un-burns her burdens:
words caveup-cavedown in her mouth;
she knows speakers telling tales of a growing town:
a specter photograph in an un-empty room.

Girl is not a vilified transaction in a ghost market.
Girl is not an abandoned deal or bargain.

She is a place. A sentence without a full stop.
She is a gong that knows its tunes in an orchestra.

Girl is not holy. She is holy.
Girl is not a halo. She is a halo.
Girl is not a weak phrase or a dying clause.

Girl is a place called Ishiowèrrè
in Owèrrè-nkwoji in Imo.
Girl is a wind,
a no-ruffled house. A ruffled house,
a surnamed place raised by Ọbashị
who gave its lands to Ibegwa
who gave its fire to Ọhaeto
who gave its river to Ogbonna.
Ogbonna passed the baton to Ezenwa
who saw everything was beautiful and
gave the lands, the fire, the river to me,
Chinụalụmọgụ.

Chinụalụmọgụ Sits on His Balcony Pretending He Is a Parcel

I sit on my balcony pretending I am a parcel.
Sometimes we surprise ourselves.
Sometimes we make for ourselves.
I teach my wounds that I can be many things,
that I can pose for moon kisses, that I can string my eloquence.
I teach myself how to dance in satin shoes.

It has been five months since I tendered
the light magnets buried in my throat; five months
now for the Polaroid memories nursing my worries.
For years, hands have been blacking out our history
and our pasts have been asking for ordinance and recalling.

I learned how to wait for twilight to understand really
that this is a terrible time to be alive,
that there is a sad dent in every love story.
I say my father's name Ezenwa, his father's name Ogbonna,
his father's father's name Ọhaeto, his father's father's father's name Ibegwa,
his father's father's father's father's name Ọbashị
to make everyone understand the things I have been denied.

Dogwood diaries shake off the dust settling on their pages.
And somewhere I read that when one prays for long,
silence becomes a prayer too. How much silence can heal,
can house the memories that indict me?

Many times I am left with the choice to think
that the best thing about being dead is freedom.
But those the dead leave behind aren't free.
I keep looking for what it means to mask our wounds;
what it takes to know excitement in celebrations.

Worries

America is anywhere you work your bones to the core to
make another very rich
—DONALD GLOVER

I saw in a movie, a boy—one with hunger—asking for
a pint of care; I saw in the movie, a boy racing after cars
with outstretched arm and his eyes begging to survive the day.

"Anywhere" is also this country, and I have been standing
for long on it to recognize the bad-bad things
the monkey's hand is doing to it.

My long-dead father wakes with me and I am shown
the ways around a twisted tree. My mother has a way of reaching
me without being near: my navel carries the weight of her fears.
Our fathers' fathers, I am worried. My fears sound like a can of nails.

The Teenager Who Became a Mother

—after the teenage mother from Ọ̀lú who survived the Unknown Gunmen

The teenager who became a mother, and who for two months survived
the unknown gunmen, had her way of feeling, seeing, and hoping.
It was her zeal that rafted her and her unborn child
through the blood-orange fire that seized into the skies.

Our fathers' fathers, she had a black-rimmed skin
that shimmered more than coal and bronze masks:
a cascade of courage never falling asleep in the sun.

She was not one-eyed or one-lipped, but wet with rivers' hems.
Her hairs were strands of broken happiness and loneliness.
Her viscera—patient as optimism and plan.

And each of the scars on her back was a memory.

When I asked if she saw anyone die during the raids,
she moved her head up and down.
She said she saw five, twenty, and even more;

that some of them drowned before her eyes; that
every day survived was accosted by gunshots;
and that the thing anyone didn't want to become was a target.

I looked into her eyes—after she had told me about her
ordeal, risks, and the rainy nights she curled under a tree—
and saw the teenager who braved everything:

she was a graveyard to them
who drowned before her eyes and
a mother who wanted her child
to not look anything like the towns of smoke.

What They Say I Do Not Carry Well

—after the raid in the outskirts of Imo State

Our fathers' fathers,
they say I do not carry my place well,
because it smells of blood and ruin,
the kind left behind on the departure of men with heavy guns.
Many times I do want to know what God, Chukwu Ọ̀kị̀ké, thinks of it,
if he still remembers the love and care in
the promise he placed on its borders.
If he can see the people on it now—bashed, broken, and weary.
People with perforated lives. People with specks of dust covering their brows.
People with sores in their dreams. People who eat their appendixes to survive.
People whose sisters and brothers never lived to see another dusk,
after an evening of flying bullets, covering the ground in red and smokes.
Sisters died in one afternoon. They had only gone to the market for food.
Their voices welling with songs were put into silence.
Brothers' hearts became canvases of pains and fear: they were
in the field playing football until their bodies were forced to disobey gravity.
Every morning I hold the map in my hands and paint butterflies on it,
to make it easier for me to remember lost names from the others.
Last night, I saw a wallpaper of Bob Marley.
His covered dreadlocks, like a halo, made him look saintly.
Bob's eyes reminded me of his music—so messianic. Every one of them.
I wish to talk to him and let him know how his lyrics lay bare here:
bare like the sea; like raw, uncut scenes from a movie.
I wish to see him and listen to what he thinks of my place.
But tell me, our fathers' fathers: am I born for this disaster? That smells of deaths?
Even Christ begged his Father to prevent his suffering at Gethsemane.
Dear God, Chukwu Ọ̀kị̀ké, I want to carry my place well.
Or maybe you live here just for one day.

A Dead Son Does Not Answer the Phone

(On January 16, 2016, two bombs exploded at the University
of Maiduguri, Nigeria, killing about . . . by VOA News)

The ground shook somewhere in Maiduguri.
Hundreds feared dead, said a reporter from an old radio sitting nearby.
A woman in the market caught the reporter's words.
She abandoned her customers and reached for
her phone held together with rubbers.
She dialed, it rang, no answer.
Two, three balls of sweat ran down her forehead.
She dialed again, it rang—
poohhhhh . . . poohhhhh . . . poohhhhhh . . .
—slower and longer to her pounding heart.
Hello Mama, the son said on picking up.
The woman rattled, *I just heard from the radio*
that there was a bomb blast over there, are you okay?
I am fine, Mama, said the son. *I am fine.*

In this place, we know too many losses.
Every day, people are running for safety. *Tufiakwa!*
All news is accompanied by something horrible:
people forcefully pulled away from their bodies.

The World Will Never Run Out of Bad News

—after the EndsARS Protest

Sometime in 2020, the *EndsARS* protest hit a climax.
People demanded for a country free from abuse and harassment.
A boy in dreadlocks, with a tattoo and on a bus, was asked
to step down and then taken to the police station on
the account of looking like a thief, a weed plug, and a fraudster.
One evening, a university's girls' hostel was raided, and
some girls were put in cuffs without any explanation.
Some, whose privacy was invaded, were tagged sex workers.
Their debit cards were confiscated and only returned after they
were forced to make transfers to an unknown bank account.
I know these too because I was once stopped on the way out
of my compound and was gun-butted for asking for a search warrant.
During the protest, our fathers' fathers, people were killed
as they waved the flag of their country, as they
requested accountability, as they showed how their
hurt carried the weight and traces of mistreatment and exploitation.
And other people, who were nowhere close to the scene
of this abomination, some residing abroad, came
online and said that nobody died. That no life was lost.
I do not know which was worse—
the murders or the denials. *Chai!*
The world will never run out of bad news,
but we must not forget these people who were killed.
I will not forget them and why they died.
To forget is akin to killing them
a second time and many times over.

Ọzụbụlụ

I have never been to Ọzụbụlụ,
but I have a friend from the town.
He said there are a few makeshifts here and there,
where men gather in the evenings and play draughts.
Cigarettes and alcohol, just like most places,
wrestle with the air in the corners of the town.
And a motel where sweats are traded stands at its border.
My friend has lived in this town all his life,
and worked as a vulcanizer until university happened.
On August 6, 2017, armed men invaded St. Philip's
Catholic Church in Ọzụbụlụ during a Sunday service
and shot dead fifteen worshippers; left many injured.
Bodies were reconfigured with openings; some brought
down halfway through their run for a cover;
some brought down on the church's altar, their blood
pooling at the base where the crucifix was stationed;
a child was caught under a pile of chairs, and meters away
from her body was her arm clinching a teddy bear.
These were people with dreams and plans.
The following day, the news stations kept silent,
as if nothing had happened anywhere.
This country has become heavier than a ship's anchor and its chains;
its mouth reeks of rotten whales; its wings are perforated with negligence.
I love this country, but it does not love me back.
I walk toward it, yet it keeps running from me.

Úgà

—after the bombardment and destruction of Úgà town by Britain, 1916

Our fathers' fathers, 42 miles away
from this homestead is a town called Úgà.
A place of warm temperature in all seasons,
and known for its Obuofor festival and Obizi spring.
Trading is its craft, and every Òrìè day,
its market swells with goods and people.
It is a town where yams are abundant, never knowing
scarcity. A town steeped in traditions, where the
Ajabu masquerade, elegant, solitary, unpleasant,
and an amazement to injustice, takes center stage.

As history has it, before 1916, Úgà was occupied by the British.
The town's people never liked their settlement,
for what was done and taken from them never sat well
in their eyes. Then, the town's people, alongside their
sacred masquerade, Ajabu, protested for many, many days
against the foreigners, telling them to their faces the ugly
things they did: the heavy taxation, the disruption of their festival,
the forceful taking of their ancestral lands, the abuse of their young
women, the selling of their young men, 16 of them known and many
others unknown, in chains and wooden yoke across the sea . . .

In 1916, in one Òrìè market day,
Úgà was bombarded and brought to ruins by
the British settlers. A hard lesson in arms and fire.
Our fathers' fathers, mothers lost their children,
fathers lost their wives, homes were wrecked,
and the town, brought to smoke and wailings.

That day was a terrible one. *Tsk!*
And because, our fathers' fathers, what happened
was unbearable, the burden too much for words,
some people fled Úgà. At night, the night bird
took the terrible things the day saw to the sky.

Monochrome Photos with Fragments in a Closet

—*after Aba Women's Riots, 1929*

One history book from the library had it
that after January 1, 1914, it became a fact
that godheads setup an order to lick dry
the pockets of districts under their control.
These godheads in the lesser name of warrant chiefs—
among them was Okugo of Oloko—questioned
every door they could find for a reassessment of
the taxable wealth of the people. The women, children,
and domestic animals now had to be counted and accounted for.
I am not one who gets scared easily, but I cannot imagine that
one morning, everyone in a district had to hide to smoke their pipes.
My distant uncle, Enyi, who died many years before
I was born and a man of a few words, then brought
down his barn in one night and told his son to sell
off its fat tubers of yam. To him, it was a better idea than
to have most of them taken away. Inside the library, I turned
a page of the book, half the page bore monochrome photos of some
women, all in a market place filled with wares: it was the year, 1929.
The story was in fragments and in the name of the market women of Aba.
On the November afternoon of that year, the market women, among
whom was Nwanyeruwa, a cousin to my distant uncle's wife,
refused the order. *Nobody counts their mothers*, she rattled.
And what followed her voice thereafter was a crowd.
The women walked the distance from their homes, farms, and kiosks,
their bodies in protest; these women, 10 thousand strong, raised
dust from the earth that even those long gone heard and stood still—
against enumerations, against these bats who only knife things.
These 10 thousand women sat on these godheads, including Okugo.

The warrant chiefs and their troops fought back with batons and guns.
Bodies fell, and the earth caught the thuds of these women's bravery.
Despite the deaths of about 55 women and many others wounded,
they sat out the order, and everything that accompanied it.
And like a church bell, that day's movement crossed borders—
from Aba to Owèrrè to Calabar and beyond.
It is many years gone now, and children perform this incident on playgrounds,
running after one another, chanting and playing Nwanyeruwa.
In the history book, I dog-eared each line pregnant with the women's voices.
I felt my arm, checking the veins carrying the echoes of that day,
because I didn't ever want to forget that in the absence of the past and
these valiant women's love and courage, I couldn't have existed.

As Seeing Is a Kind of Brightness

—*Nigeria-Biafra War in retrospect, 1967–70*

a. Remembrances are sometimes dazed lilies,
sometimes laughter and smiles,
sometimes regrets and losses.

b. Many months ago, as we sat together at the balcony one evening,
you, kinsman, told me of the hurt that has weighed heavily
on your heart to this day. I can see it in your eyes and hear it
in your voice; it still stings, sharper than iodine on an open wound.

c. Now, you dream and see field flowers in sepia.
You feel the rise and fall of hostility in the eyes of those you
birthed and in the hearts of those they birthed too.

d. Remembrances are sometimes strung
together by missiles and grenades and tanks.
They wake fathers every morning with fear and retribution.
They sing lullabies to mothers every night with dread and terror.

e. That particular day when your school suddenly
closed down, it was 1968. The air was filled with sirens.
Your teacher hid under the class table, her hands clasping her ears.
Your classmates scaled through windows and scampered for the door out.
You were eight years old and hurried home
through the screaming crowd and stampede;
through burning and smoking streets; through blistered walls
and opened bodies—everywhere turning into atrophies and ruins.

f. On opening the door into your house, there was your father still in a
corner staring at you with shocked eyes; he was
drenched in his blood, with a knife stuck to his head.
In another corner was your mother with her tummy wide open,
and your brother, no, your sister slipping out, still corded to her.
You ran outside, running and running and cursing into the air till
no more words were left in your voice.

g. Many years have gone by and everything
that happened that day is still green in your head.
As seeing is a kind of brightness,
you wonder how you lived all through these years,
bearing the heavy memory and loss, bearing on
your lips, *never again to fire, never again to blood and death.*

Okụzụ

*Abuchi Modilim, a man of pun, goodness, and height told me this story.
It was his story, his uncle's story and his father's story. I was so touched
that I decided to be part of it through a retelling.*

Our fathers' fathers, about 120 miles away from this homestead,
there is a place called Okụzụ, where years ago, brothers, sisters and children
never suffered from the loss of the seasons; where families, all of
them gallant, never knew loneliness; they knew the language of farming.

This place remained this way for years, until one afternoon in 1967,
bombs from the sky found their way to it and the villages nearby.
And sank houses and playgrounds. Sank schools, barns, and farms.
Everywhere sang of smoke, wailings, dust, wounds, and deaths.
One man, in the name of Nwankwo from Okụzụ, blessings upon his name,
who went to the market in Òtùòchà, a nearby village, to buy some food was
    in the mess.
His limb flew off his body, and landed somewhere, shattered and in pieces.
This ruined him for life: it affected how he walked, affected his hearing.
He lived his life after the war retelling the story to whoever cared to listen.

After the bombings, Ekeokwu who heard the news a day later while
at work, abandoned everything he was doing and rode his bicycle down
to Òtùòchà, searching for Nwankwo, his brother. But he couldn't find him,
not among the survivors, not among those in the corner crying their losses,
not in the ruins, not even among the lifeless and still bodies lying on the streets.
He was told that some people who were seriously injured by the bomb blasts
were taken to Énugwú for treatment. With an address, Ekeokwu entered the
road and rode 118 miles from Òtùòchà to Énugwú. It was a desperate journey
on a bicycle, hoping that what he feared would never become imminent.

He got to Énugwú, and found his brother, Nwankwo, in the hospital.
Nwankwo, once a chancellor of sparks, was traumatized and gnashing in pain.
Ekeokwu hugged his brother, relieved that what the road and the rode miles
brought to his thoughts never happened. Thereafter, he carried his brother
and placed him on his bicycle, and rode back to Okụzụ to care for him.

Our fathers' fathers, the past's iron bell must never tire,
but in this story, there was beauty, consolation, joy, and love
between brothers. Love risked all: it was never a confession but an act,
it foresaw hope and acted on it. In this story, hope sprouted into flowers.

At the Darien Gap

—on Africans dying on crossing Darien Gap to reach the U.S.

Dear kinsman, Nwanne m, you remember Obinna,
the son of Obierika? Yes, that's the one. Our fathers' fathers,
Obinna's mouth now wants to forget the breadth of this country,
forget how he once rolled into it and swallowed its lynching rains,
because it has become a tiger tigering the people in it.
What place pirouettes the things and people in it into ashes?
What place burns into skins and says that one is an embodiment
and a reflection of things cracked and squashed?
One time, a boy saw Obinna and stuffed his greetings into his back pockets.
Two hurts on a boiling spot are never unlike poles. and will never attract.
This country does not know how to hold the people in it—histories stitched
    in loops.
It fills dreams with flowers grown at the graveside—truckloads of broken stars.
It has no name for yesterday's reflections and today's possibilities. no full stop.
At the Darien Gap, Obinna's legs want to become a portico of run. run. run is
    not a verb.
Run is a name for projected safety. A name for stars and moon.
At the Darien Gap, his tongue wants to lose the taste of this country,
lose the taste of its metals that spread into mass graves, for what place
folds its night and day into litanies of grieves? What place grows people backward?
grows fire and shells? And words from its news headlines, radios and televisions
are lists of found and unknown limbs and bones. This country knows too
    much loss.
It knows corridors in red. Knows walls graffitied by mangled bodies. And burnt
fleshes, the color of baked tangerines. At the Darien Gap, Obinna wants everything
wrong with this country as forces doused at the feet of memories.

DEAR HOPE

My mother often says, *you think something hard,*
you give it powers.

One day I envisioned my niece
playing with a fishing hook and hurting herself.

Days later, my niece lost a finger playing with a fishing hook,
and I blamed myself for thinking it.

Finding

A

Dear hope, I accept your
embrace for this place, my place
of birth, and everywhere else, just as
the sea shares its love with the shore.

B

Here on billboards, worries and grief stretch themselves,
except for a particular one bearing a face smiling up his pockets
and making the lands he governs throw up wilting roses.
A boy, with an empty bowl, picks up a stone and aims at it.
Instead of reverberation, a careless fuel tanker—supposed
to be on road ban—cripples down and heaves the boy
into a corner: splintered, baked black, and bloody.

C

Our fathers' fathers, how long does one have to hold hope here before
it manifests into better systems, into a beautiful landscape
collaged by blooming orchids so people will walk through it and marvel?

D

Dear hope, when I say I take your embrace just as the sea shares its
glorious affection with its shore, I am trying to find. Love. and. Home.
A place bigger than fire. Bigger than bombs. Bigger than mis-
management. Bigger than aching jaws and the monkey's hand.
A place as beautiful and marvellous as the moment when a sparrow lifts.

ÌkwÌkwĺî, Sweet Night Bird, by the Lamp on a Dim-Lighted Street

Sing to me. Sing.
Pull me off the forlorn-filled box with your songs.
I have been touched more than I can bear by the monkey's hand.
I am a man who has refused to grow reversed.
I am a man left in the middle of a dream.
Sing to me dear night bird. Sing.
I didn't walk this far to become a twisted rubber tree on a twisted road.
I do not want to agree that my story is an abandoned Tesla,
or an abandoned shirt in a girlfriend's house.
Sing to me. O, bird of the mystic and sight.
Pull me off this swing that swings me unsteadily.
I am a man left in the middle of a road.
Dear sweet night bird, sing to this man on
a dim-lighted street by his homestead.

Ọbashị

I carry your name, our fathers' fathers, everywhere I go
because it means to live with purpose, together, and with love.
I remember the great things you did in the past,
and your deeds enshrined, laced and celebrated in myths.
I know how grand your knowledge walked into the mystic.
You knew the ways of being here and being there,
the nooks of astral travel and bilocation.

One story goes that many, many years ago,
a neighboring town's merchant dealing in irons and crafted pistols
had a daughter who went to sleep one night and could not wake up.
This went on for two days, though she still had life in her.
Messengers were sent, calling for masters of healing and revival—
but what could a wind do when there was the whirlwind,
what weight could a goat carry when there was a buffalo?

All the mouths that heard spoke for what they knew,
and each sentence, each phrase, each clause they carried echoed Ọbashị.
Then came you, our fathers' father, answering to our name,
to the art that never relented when it was called upon.
You told the merchant that it was Àfọ̀ day; that because it was a
great day, her daughter would be fine—Alandiiche agreed to this.

In a room in the merchant's house, where the girl lay,
you sat by her side, legs crisscrossed, closed your eyes,
and everything became dilated—it was not an emptiness,
but a box waiting to be filled with light. The sky leaned
closer while your body journeyed to where no feet could go.

You found the girl beneath Akpu, the silk cotton tree,
at the crossroads, the veil between the living and the dead.

Two hours passed, and whispers bloomed, fibrous utterings and shuffling:
the birds flicked their wings; dogs grew weary of bones and their own licking.
Mouths fluttered, bending to the pages of doubt and distrust.

Five hours passed, and when you opened your eyes, the girl opened hers.
As the room's door creaked open, there were heads gathered outside,
towering and pushing through, eager not to miss any unfolding.
With you, Ọbashị was the merchant's daughter. In her fullness and breath.
Blessings upon her name. Ọbashị, the son of Idụma, what no one could do,
    you did.

After that day, all the eyes, heads, and mouths that witnessed
took to the ears they could find—saying that
what was lost could be found; what was bent could be unbent.

Confession

In everything, I speak for myself
because I, alone, know where the bats
inside me are trembling and choking my lineage.

I stand before a mirror and am marveled
by the things I have refused to become.

I have refused to become a collared dog eating its own
tail, refused to be that man cut down in his age of ripeness,
refused to be the man who forgot his kindred—Okoro Ọbashị,
the lifeblood of my lineage; and refused to become the favorite
dress awaiting a never-happening special occasion.

I'll dip my hands in Ọhia, the ancestral river,
and wait till it lets me know what I am yet to know.

Chinụalụmọgụ's Therapist Kept
Smiling at His Tricks

I visited my therapist
and stretched as I could
to familiarize myself again
with my excesses and wounds.
My therapist listened to me.
I towed a string of want and grew
passages where my father's voice asked me
for the meaning of forgetting.
I have never wanted to forget,
but I have faltered in remembering.
I told my therapist each time a butterfly
kissed the nape of my happiness,
I hopped into a fluorescent-filled dream
and saw the faces of people who harmed me,
and I wanted them to speak to me.
Tears have been the wools softening my burdens.
I told my therapist that sometimes my loneliness sat
outside of me: moments I couldn't avoid without
flooding my throat with wine-filled glasses.
I told my therapist that my to-do list had it that I would
unravel the parentheses of past tears.
She weighed my failings and said it was the doings of *Agwu*.

The truth is: I have been throwing stones
at the guidelines meant to settle
the dust rising in my head.

I always worried. Worried about things not going as they should.
The sun dulls and the story about privileged complaints rises.
I really want to be happy.
I really want everything poking me to un-poke.

Web

a. I touch the almanac of worries sitting in my head.
I want them to know light. And also know grace.
It's not as if I know anything else to do with the worries except to worry.

b. In an essay, Achebe said if you want to understand an
Igbo person and how life has treated him,
check the names of his children.
You will find his worries, hopes, his joys
and sorrows; his grievances. Even his fears.

c. Sometimes it's good to feed our fears.
I feed mine just to see them look overfed.
I want my fears to take on their tongue.

d. Kinsman, Nwanne m, do throw away the sleep gathering
in your eyes. Remember that when bad things are happening, we spit on
the ground, *tueh!* The shame goes to our ancestors. But we will not allow it.
That's why we are here. Throw away the sleep gathering in your eyes.

e. In the nights, when I look up at the full moon,
I wonder why it's so appealing like a well-decorated food.

f. There's something about people and their spirits
that keeps a place going, that keeps a place buzzing.
It's like the way the mechanisms of an engine engineers the engine.

g. I often forget what it feels like eating with bare hands,
often forget that I was once a boy who hunted grasshoppers in the farm,
often forget why I left home for the university across many seas.

h. It's not as if I know anything else to do with the worries except to worry
I want them to know light. And also know grace.
I touch the almanac of worries sitting in my head.

A Page from Chinụalụmọgụ's Diary

This thing I have looks like a mouth.
No, it is not a mouth, it's an opening.
My mother puts prayers inside my head. To be my guide.
A young man gave me a microphone one afternoon.
He wanted me to be heard.
I screamed *Love* into it and everyone ran away.
It didn't come out well, he said. *Try another word.*
So I said *Live*—
No one ran away. But everyone stared
into one another's eyes, questioning the torn
sandals left behind by lovers and the monkey's hand.
I left the young man and everyone around for
the waterfront to see and weigh my reflection.
Once, my uncle gave me a bottle of beer
and being a man of a few sentences, he said:
rinse your mouth with it. Thereafter
he took me to the balcony,
Now that you see clearly,
can you see how the moon is also the sun?

Foregrounding

One day, after a lecture where a professor
taught the tricks of foregrounding,
I understood that the obsession I was unable to locate
inside of me wasn't inside of me.
I was looking at the wrong place.
And to a fault, I was confused until I wasn't.

The thing is that the obsession was never inside of me.
It was outside. And I am looking at it now.
Looking at it on the mangoes sitting
like 4 weeks old rabbits from Tibet inside my opened fridge.

To make you understand, our fathers' fathers, I'll explain:
I eat lots of mangoes—those sweet-sweet gods of sweetness.
They see us from the shops where they are gathered by sellers.
They see us from their posts on the trees.
They see us when they leave their posts for the ground.
They see us and draw us to themselves.
Mangoes, those sweet-sweet gods of sweetness, draw us to themselves.
They keep telling us to get them, to buy them, to eat them.
They are obsessed with us, with me, with our mouths.
They are obsessed with us just like every other thing that can obsess.

Falling Oranges

As a young boy, I was told that I could be anything
I wanted. I have carried this with great expectations,
and have been opening many doors—and wrong ones too.

I have been studying algorithms to see if in
any way I can get the future to talk to me.
I want to know the insides of things.
I want to know about effect before its cause:
it is one way one can catch falling oranges before
they hit the ground and open their bellies to the world.

In this place of my birth, I pray for good roads,
for good hospitals and schools, for good food and drugs,
for electricity, for better take-home pay, for competence
and for a good night's sleep, safety and my entitlements.

I see grasses by the village roads, dancing under the passing
breeze, it's easy to say things and hardest to understand.

A Gift from Ọlisa Eloka, the One from Umuchu, to His Dearest Friend, Chinụalụmọgụ, Who Received It on the Afternoon of the Third Day After His Traditional Marriage to Mmesoma

—dedicated to C and M (2022—0000)

I
See you now, your two faces,
cutting palm fronds of love from the wild.
See you now, leaping over the m̀bụ̀ze of ache.
And who is to say what good fortune would
come after this?

See you now in the morning of your lives,
plucking November tangerines from the sky.
The monkey's hand will never near your home.
The sirens come and the masquerades,
suddenly altruistic, waltz
and everyone hums to the epitaph of
a story at birth. A story unhalved.

II
I shall retain you in memory and in forever,
two beautiful silhouettes locked in a full embrace at golden hour,
billowing in the evening breeze.

You, Chinụa, are the priest
and she, Mmesoma, is the sun,
dispelling the eclipse from your eyes.

As the incense burns,
worship yourselves
to the end of your lives;

I will sing you a hymn
and drum her a dance.

III
I break this kòlà in your names
and it splits into four lobes.
The good spirits harken.

Mercy

Chukwu biko zienu, make my wants closer as I go for them.
I have learned to ask for your mercy by having
mercy on myself. I am open to the grace that begets flourishing
until I know sufficiency. I am open to the wisdom
of first saying *I am sorry* because it's a greater
answer than nailing anger into the wall.
I want to have a daughter first. And when she grows, will someday
want me to point out the things she may not understand about adulthood.
Give me the grace to do the needful, to answer rightly.
Chukwu biko zienu, let restraint and patience find me as I find them,
so I can teach myself and friends well enough about tenderness.
Biko zienu, give me the grace to live well and with care
even when my pockets and bones are saying otherwise.
And if I ever go hungry, do not let anyone feed me poison.
It has been long I stopped blaming the robin shooting night nails at me;
it has been long I stopped blaming the arrows opening
my healed wounds. I want to welcome the breeze in the field
into my home. I have figured out how much of your light
I need to unravel the serpents untooling the gearbox of
my beauty. Chukwu biko zienu, I want to have an unmatchable steeze;
I also want to have money, just enough money to match the steeze.
I promise not to shame my enemies or anybody with it.
I only want to live well, biko zienu. I want to live
well because I deserve to live well and afford good
things. Chukwu biko zienu. Biko zienu.

Clarity

I search for the clarity of the things I do not understand.
Till now, I have never understood the proverbial
speech made by my maternal grandfather,
Iduu Ambrose Ezedinobi Ngejeme, after he gifted me a coat.
He said, *my son, may this gift be more to you than what it has been to me.*
My maternal grandfather was a business man and long dead now.
I look at his picture where his smile is a cone basking in the sun
to see in what ways it would help me understand what I might have missed.
I look up and there are cranes, measuring their
wings with the breath of the blue sky.
And I know these cranes would tend to their blessings at the shores,
familiar gesture drawing me close to what is important from what is not.
That is grace. And one of my friends often says that grace is a thing
that never opens itself anyhow to anyone. But I know
that having grace is a matter of being able to chase out
the ugly things done by the monkey's hand in this country.
It is time I valued my indifference.
It is time I recognized certain things and why my life journey
sometimes looks like a rabbit in a trap.
I want my mind delivered peacefully from what
I do not know about the anagrams of tomorrow;
I want to understand what my maternal grandfather
meant in his proverbial speech on gifting me a coat.

On Chinụalụmọgụ Once Living
in Lincoln, Nebraska

Our fathers' fathers,
I once lived in Lincoln and here is what I think of it:

"It was curiosity that led me to you, Lincoln.
You city. City of touch and tease,
immaculate, foxy, and reeved in a gallery of vintage.
Reeved in red, ease, unease, and corn fields.
With you, I was made to drift toward reason
and still hold onto faith and resilience.
With you, I discovered how much it meant to not be
liked by people around me and who flashed me fake smiles.
One time like that, you mischaracterized me
for being a human who genuinely cared, rode the test track
rightly, and was simply doing what any considerate human
would do—buying loaves of bread and sharing every slice.
Lincoln, you modern-Emmett-Till-ed me.
What does my passport mean to you, Lincoln?
In one hot afternoon, a black lady I met down
the street gifted me a nod. It took me hours to
understand that the nod was also an acknowledgment.
The following day, I gifted a young man on a skating
board double nods as a sign of sharing and aptitude.
Lincoln, you were privileged to have me submerged
in these conflicting experiences with you.
You many times said I had an accent,
but what I really heard was that you had a bad ear.
What does my passport mean to you, Lincoln?
Every memory gained was a tiger claw survived.

Every scar(e) survived was another day attained.
Lincoln—you city of touch, tease, and unease;
you city beyond evaluation and maturity.
I must confess again: it was curiosity that led me to you."

Forgiveness

Never understood how free
I could be until I emptied
the stones piled in my head,
eyes, and heart.
I grow a flower
for each moment I forgive.
A bird on a pole
drops guano
down on my shoulder
and I make from it
a mosaic of laughter.
There is a road running
across my dreams,
this road where there are
no grudges and bumps,
a boy walks on it,
drawing the moonlight
over his footprints.
For years, I have harbored
a can full of nails fronting
the past and people who hurt me—
it is like a man holding a knife
against his umbilical cord.

A Call's Dusk

Our fathers' fathers, I Chinụalụmọgụ,
don talk as e dey do me.
I have said what I must.
É kwùgò m kā-òsì èmé m.
I have said what I know.
I have named the monkey's hand monkeying us badly.
I have shown the places where I am itched.
In the age of my ripeness, I'll not avoid living,
so that the good things promised at my birth
will deliver perfectly their goodness in my life.
Our fathers' fathers,
give us the needed to un-monkey the
monkey's hand monkeying us badly, and even
the monkey's hand yet to monkey us.
As I unbow my head and rise to my feet, our fathers' fathers,
may anywhere my name is mentioned be to our reverence and of great things.
Chukwu Ọ̀kị̀ké, clear this life path filled with difficulties and wrongdoings.
Our fathers' fathers, be with me. Guide us.
Let my Chi always hover around me. And fight for me.
It is the meaning of my name—Chinụalụmọgụ.
Chukwu Ọ̀kị̀ké, be with me when I am at the front.
Be with me when I am at the back.
Wherever I am and wherever I go, be with me.
In Èké, Òrìè, Àfọ̀, Nkwò, be with me, be with our kindred.

               Iseee!

               Dear kinsman, Nwanne m,
               it is now your turn.

"Chukwu" or "Chukwu Ọ̀kịké" is the greatest force, creator, and God of all existence in the Igbo cosmology. He manifests as Agwu, Amadioha, Anyanwu, Ala, and Chi to serve different purposes.

"Chinụalụmọgụ" is my first name in full (the Igbo people have "Chi," a personal and spiritual guide that descends from the great God, Chukwu) which loosely means "Chi fight for me."

"Alandiiche" is the domain of the Ancestors in the Igbo cosmology.

"Chukwu biko zienu" is an Igbo expression for "God please."

"Nwanne m" is an Igbo word for sibling, brother, sister, cousin, or kinsman.

"Èké, Òrìè, Àfọ̀, Nkwọ̀" are the Igbo people's days, as well as their market days.

"tueh!"and "tufiakwa!" are Igbo expressions for "God forbid."

"Ékwè" is an Igbo musical instrument which the English Language calls "Slit Drum."

"Ìjelè" is a type of Igbo Masquerade: big and highly decorated. And "Ìzàgà" is the tallest Igbo Masquerade, known for its humor and showing off.

For my lineage, I learned that about 400 years ago, a man named Ikaigbo from Agbo, now part of Delta State, had a grandson named Ishigbo, who resettled in the present Owèrrè-nkworji in Imo State, which is where my family originates. Ishigbo fathered Owèrrè, who fathered Ishiowèrrè, who fathered Idụma. Idụma fathered Ọbashị, who fathered Ibegwa. Ibegwa fathered Ohaeto, followed by Ogbonna, then Ezenwa, and finally, me. This was told to me by De Amarachi Ndubuisi, who got it from De Odoenyi Ndubuisi, who in turn got the story from Da Uma-Ọbashị.

"ụmụ Obashi" and "Okoro Obashi" mean Children/Offspring of Obashi. For this collection, I chose to focus exclusively on exploring my lineage from Ọbashị, the first son of Idụma. The position of the head of the clan and kindred was passed down to me through the lineage of the first son.

In the poem "Color" the lines "Death makes us protest the fact of death. / Is there any logic to death, to grief, to after death?" are from an essay by Teju Cole in his book, *Black Paper: Writing in a Dark Time*.

"SARS" is the Special Anti-Robbery Squad, a unit of the Nigerian Police known for its notoriety and abuse of Nigerian citizens.

"Mbùze" is the Igbo word for erosion.

"ÌkwÌkwÍi" is an Igbo word for owl. And "Ńzụ̀" is the Igbo word for "Kaolin" or "Calabash chalk."

In the poem "There Is a New Philosophy Now Called *Kwechiri, to Persevere*," the line "*No gree for anybody, sister. But, remember also that Keke driver / wey face trailer for road no dey shout 'no gree for anybody' / Na die be that!*" is a Nigerian pidgin which loosely means "a cab driver dare not seek for space with a 10-wheeler driver on the highway, because he knows death would be inevitable."

"Kwechiri" and its other derivatives, like "no gree for anybody," used in this collection mean "to Persevere."

In the poem "Itches," part 1 is influenced by 1 Corintians 13:11 (KJV) and Isaiah 5:20 (KJV).

The poem "What I Said to God, Chukwu Ọ̀kị̀ké" has an adjusted line from Romeo Oriogun's "Departure" from *Sacrament of Bodies*. Also the poem "What They Say I Do Not Carry Well" borrows a line from him.

The poem "On Chinụalụmọgụ once Living in Lincoln, Nebraska" has some adjusted expressions from Peter Drury's exaltation of Cristiano Ronaldo on his return to Manchester United Football Club.

"I don talk as e dey do me" is Nigerian pidgin for "This is how I feel."

"É kwùgò m kā-òsì èmé m" is Igbo language for "This is how I feel."

"Iseee!" is an Igbo expression for "Affirming" or "Let it be so."

In the poem "A Call's Dusk," the slightly adjusted line "In the age of my ripeness, I'll not avoid living" is from "The Post Chant" in Ezenwa-Ọhaeto's *The Chants of a Minstrel*.

A few of the poems in this collection were part of my Chapbook, *The Teenager Who Became My Mother*, published by Sevhage, 2020.

Olisa Eloka's Whatsapp statuses were useful, a bit of them with permission found their way, reformed, into this collection.

I am indebted to my father, Ezenwa-Ọhaeto, for his words, craft, and teachings through his works and poetry collections. Respect, respect to you, Bàbá; my two hands are in the air, hailing.

Logotherapy
Mukoma Wa Ngugi

Breaking the Silence: Anthology
of Liberian Poetry
Edited by Patricia Jabbeh Wesley

When the Wanderers Come Home
Patricia Jabbeh Wesley

Seven New Generation African
Poets: A Chapbook Box Set
Edited by Kwame Dawes
and Chris Abani
(Slapering Hol)

Eight New-Generation African
Poets: A Chapbook Box Set
Edited by Kwame Dawes
and Chris Abani
(Akashic Books)

New-Generation African Poets:
A Chapbook Box Set (Tatu)
Edited by Kwame Dawes
and Chris Abani
(Akashic Books)

New-Generation African Poets:
A Chapbook Box Set (Nne)
Edited by Kwame Dawes
and Chris Abani
(Akashic Books)

New-Generation African Poets:
A Chapbook Box Set (Tano)
Edited by Kwame Dawes
and Chris Abani
(Akashic Books)

New-Generation African Poets:
A Chapbook Box Set (Sita)
Edited by Kwame Dawes
and Chris Abani
(Akashic Books)

New-Generation African Poets:
A Chapbook Box Set (Saba)
Edited by Kwame Dawes
and Chris Abani
(Akashic Books)

New-Generation African Poets:
A Chapbook Box Set (Nane)
Edited by Kwame Dawes
and Chris Abani
(Akashic Books)

To order or obtain more information on these or other University of
Nebraska Press titles, visit nebraskapress.unl.edu. For more information
about the African Poetry Book Series, visit africanpoetrybf.unl.edu.

www.ingramcontent.com/pod-product-compliance
Ingram Content Group UK Ltd.
Pitfield, Milton Keynes, MK11 3LW, UK
UKHW021811091125
464887UK00001B/32

9 781496 244703